GW00758885

Overhead and Over Here

The story of American military aviation in Northern Ireland during the Second World War

Ernie Cromie

Published in 2015 and reprinted
in 2017 and 2020 by
Northern Ireland War Memorial,
21 Talbot Street, Belfast BT1 2LD
www.niwarmemorial.org

ISBN 978-0-9929301-5-8

The rights of Ernie Cromie as the
author of this work have been
asserted in accordance with the
Copyright, Design and Patents
Act 1988.

Design by John McMillan

Printed by
GPS Colour Graphics Ltd

Acknowledgements

The author and the Council of the Northern Ireland War Memorial would
like to thank; Warren R Bradley, Richard Doherty, Ciaran Elizabeth Doran,
Victoria Gibson, Jenny Haslett, Anneliese Kruger, Will Lindsay, Kerry
McIvor, John McMillan, Pat McMillan, Jonny McNee, William H Nance,
Douglas Rough, Bryan Rutledge, Charles H Stover and Robert Wilson.
Special thanks are paid to the staff of the US Air Force Historical Research
Agency and US National Archives & Records Administration.

Picture Credits

NIWM would like to thank the Ulster Aviation Society for permission to
reproduce photographs and memorabilia from their collection. Additional
thanks is given to; Roy Dunham, Anneliese Kruger, Lockheed Martin, Clive
Moore, William H Nance, Alistair Payne, Charles H Stover, Andy Thomas,
US Air Force Historical Research Agency, US National Archives & Records
Administration and Guy Warner.

Second World War and World War Two

There is sometimes confusion between the terms *Second World War* and *World
War Two*. The term *Second World War* relates to the period 3rd September 1939
to 15th August 1945, while *World War Two* is the Americanisation which
relates to a different timespan – 7th December 1941 (when America became
involved in the War, after the attack on Pearl Harbor) to 15th August 1945.

The term *Second World War* is used throughout this book as it is the term
recommended by The British Commission for Military History, and British
publishing houses.

American Spelling

American spelling is used in this book when something specifically relates to
the USA or the American Forces, for example *Pearl Harbor*.

Lough Neagh Partnership is delighted to be involved in the reprint of this
publication which showcases the important role of the airfields around Lough
Neagh in the Second World War. Much of the built, natural and cultural
heritage of the area reflects this massive impact. This continuing partnership
between Lough Neagh Partnership, the Northern War Memorial and the
Ulster Aviation Society began with a successful conference in the autumn of
2018 aptly titled Overhead and Underfoot: Legacies of the Second World War
around Lough Neagh. This publication is a major contributor to that
constantly revealing story.

Dr Liam Campbell
Built and Cultural Heritage Officer with the Lough Neagh Landscape Partnership
November 2020

A founding principle of the Northern Ireland War Memorial is the recognition of the links and friendship forged between the United States of America and Northern Ireland during the Second World War.

One of Northern Ireland's most important contributions to the war effort was that it effectively acted as a staging platform for Allied forces. Like many other parts of the United Kingdom, Northern Ireland played host to large numbers of American service personnel training for major theatres of combat such as North Africa and later the D-Day landings in Normandy. Most people now think of the GIs, or the US Navy in Belfast Lough anchorage, but there were Americans flying overhead also. Many new airfields were built, most importantly, the major US Army Air Forces repair base at Langford Lodge.

A very interesting perspective arises when we start to consider the war in the air, 1939–1945. It all happened astonishingly quickly after the element of the air first became a theatre of war at all. Just 36 years had passed since the Wright Brothers' first manned, powered flight in 1903.

What truly extraordinary progress, therefore, took the world of military aviation from frail biplanes to the exploits of the formidable aircraft and their pilots and ground support personnel outlined so vividly in these pages. No surer guide exists to these epic times in Northern Ireland's wartime history and the strong bond with the United States' forces than Ernie Cromie, for no less than 30 years Chairman of the Ulster Aviation Society and a valued member of the Council of the Northern Ireland War Memorial.

This splendid publication chronicles another vital aspect of Northern Ireland's contribution to the cause of Allied victory in the Second World War.

Ian Wilson
Chairman, Northern Ireland War Memorial

Charles Bray
929 Lakeside Pl.
Chicago, Ill.

"Good Luck Jack"
Frank Pryor from
Calif. where the rain
shines year round

Chas. R. Cummings
968 Grande Vista
Los Angeles.
Calif.

"Best of Luck"
Don Track
Monocacy Sta.
Pennsylvania

W. O. Ahlson
Quijotoa, Arizona.

"Jackson" thanks for all the
advice about "wimmen"
U.S.A.

Bill Bayne
932 West 69th St.
Los Angeles

Louis Schummer
1611 N. Hudson
Hollywood Calif.

To Jack
you ought to be
in pictures. Good
luck and thanks for
your hospitality.
R.R. Bertrand.
5707 La mirada Ave
Hollywood

Dwight "Tiny" Martin
1409½ - 16th st
Sacramento, Calif.

Louis W. Marshall
838 East Washington st.
Morris, Illinois.

Loads of Luck Fella.
Bill Albrecht
New York City

H. "Chet" Kauffman
320 So. Broad St.
Lititz
Penna.

Chas. C. Cargile
Gainsville, Georgia

B.B. Davis
130 Quebec Pl N.W.
Washington, D.C.

Dick Rowe
14 Warwick St
Wollaston
Mass
WOT YOU MAKIN' JACKIE?

Tulsa, Oklahoma

Curtis Hutacher
68 East Central Ave
Wayne, N.J.

William Thomas Houston Jr.
#520 Chew Street
Allentown, Pennsylvania
"China Joe" Shanghai

Don Crilly
844 Terrace Ave
Colton, Calif

考 仕 頓
南中國邊防巡邏隊

Robert L. Baker (CIVILIAN!)
6203-B Stafford Ave,
Huntington Park Calif.
Best of Luck, "Cyclone."

W.J. Long.
4001 Duval.
Houston, Texas.

"TO THE GREAT LOVER"
"TIME WILL TELL"
VERON E. LONG
14945 MOORPARK ST
SHERMAN OAKS
CALIFORNIA

Van S. Allen
North Hollywood
California

Roy Robinson
1363 Findlay Ave
New York 56 N.Y.

Frank Trunks
1733 So. Cheyenne
Tulsa 5, Oklahoma

Bob Wherry
Stockton, Calif.

Steve, Beienburg
1008 N. 49
Seattle, Washington

John Watkins
358 W. Cedar
Burbank, Calif

Norm N. Forms
637 N. Heliotrope
Los Angeles, Calif.

Michael J. Madden
1738 El Cerrito

H. MOZART ST

Vincent B. Johnson
2105 Pioneer Rd

Arnold Bothe
875 N. Mozart
Chicago, Illinois

CONTENTS

Hawaii, Guam, Wake Targets For Jap Assault

CANANDAIGUA REPOSITORY
Founded 1797
CANANDAIGUA MESSENGER
Founded 1802
THE DAILY MESSENGER
Founded 1907

The Daily Messenger

ONTARIO COUNTY

A COUNTY PAPER FOR ONTARIO COUNTY PEOPLE

The Weather
Light snow with rising tem-eratures this afternoon and night. Tuesday snow and cold

Established in 1797. Vol. 144.—No. 288. CANANDAIGUA, N. Y., MONDAY, DECEMBER 8, 1941. Single Copy, 3 C

U. S. DECLARES WAR ON JAPAN

West Virginia, Carrier, Langley Reported Sunk

By the Associated Press

Japanese raiders struck soon after dawn Sunday. Hawaii, Wake, Guam, the Pehilippines, Malaya and Hong Kong, all were attacked in swift succession with high explosives and machine guns and Japanese troops invaded Thailand.

Two Jap raiders were reported shot down in the attack upon Hawaii. There was a report also that a Japanese aircraft carrier had been sunk in a naval engagement off Hawaii.

U. S. Sinkings Mount

From official and unofficial sources, some from the Japanese and their axis allies, grew a picture of the tolls:

Broadcast rumors that the U. S. battleship West Virginia had been sunk; the Oklahoma set afire and the carrier Langley damaged.

The U. S. transport Gen. Hugh Scott sunk 1,600 miles from Manila.

A lumber laden transport torpedoed 1,300 miles west of San Francisco.

The liner President Harding, now a transport, seized or sunk in the Yangtze river, near Shanghai.

Garrison Disarmed

The 63 man U. S. garrison at Tientsin, China, disarmed.

Shanghai's International Settlement seized by the Japanese, the U. S. gunboat Wake captured and British gunboat destroyed.

British colony of Hongkong and the U. S. Island of Guam bombed. Guam was reported to be surrounded with an oil reservoir and a hotel set ablaze.

Fifty persons were estimated in a Manila radio broadcast to have been killed in the Philippines in the attacks on Davau, Camp Ord and Clarke field, the largest U. S. army airbase of the Philippines. There was a report also that Japanese parachute troops had landed on the island.

Planes Hit Davao

Thirteen planes took part in the attack on Davao and inflicted some damage, the official announcement said.

Seventeen raiders were reported to have struck at Baguio.

The mayor of Davao reported later that the Japanese had made a second assault on Davao and had attacked a U. S. aircraft carrier in the bay.

One Japanese plane was said to have been shot down in Davao Bay, but the result of the reported attack on the aircraft carrier was not clear.

Everything Under Control

Francis B. Sayre, American high commissioner in the Philippines, meanwhile declared that the situation was "well in hand."

"Japan without warning attacked America," Sayre declared. "The constituted authorities have the situation well in hand. There is no need for anxiety. With quiet determination and courage the Philippine American people will show the stuff that's in them.

Reports reached here meanwhile that the Japanese also had attacked the U. S.-owned Island of Guam, some 1,400 miles east of the Philippines.

Admiral Thomas C. Hart, commander of the U. S. Asiatic fleet, announced that a small contingent of American Marines stationed at Peiping had been forced to surrender to the Japanese and that the American gunboat Wake at Shanghai likewise had been compelled to surrender.

"There was nothing else they could do," Admiral Hart said ...

Alaska Alert to Possible Attack

ANCHORAGE, Alaska (AP) — Alaska prepared today, alert to the possibility Japanese warships may swing northward from the battle at Hawaii.

All over the far-flung territory the Alaska defense command readied its newly-established bases for possible attack. The navy put its entire territorial establishment on a ready-for-action basis.

Army officers, declining to permit quotation, admitted Japanese warships might come this way in a northward circle on their route back toward Japan from Hawaii.

Street lights and commercial signs were darkened in Anchorage to make attack more difficult and to conserve power for military uses.

Maj. Gen. Simon Buckner, heading the Alaska defense command asked that it be continued at least a week.

General Buckner summoned all service men back from leaves and furloughs and declared all defense positions were fully manned. Army guards were stationed at offices of the Alaska communications system, army-operated radio link between territorial points and the United States proper. Red Cross units and homeguards were assigned stations.

Long War With U. S. Cited by Premier

BERLIN (AP) — DNB reported today that Japanese Prime Minister General Hideki Tojo had broadcast a message to his people warning them that they must be prepared for a long war with the United States and that the fate of the Japanese empire hung in the balance.

Tojo placed responsibility for the conflict upon the United States, according to Domei, accusing Washington of making wholly unacceptable demands upon Japan.

"In order to destroy her opponents and establish a new order in East Asia, the Japanese people must count on a long war," Tojo was quoted as saying. "The rise or decline of the Japanese empire and all of East Asia is dependent upon the outcome."

Jap Surface Craft Flee Before British

SINGAPORE (AP) — An official report from the Northern Malaya front said today that all Japanese surface craft fled at high speed under British fire after leaving a few troops on the beaches. The troops were heavily machine-gun...

Asks For War With Japan

PRESIDENT FRANKLIN D. ROOSEVELT

Hitler Seeks Quick End To Russo Fight

LONDON (AP) — Soviet troops attacking in sub-zero cold were reported today to have crushed German positions at two points above Moscow and wiped out two divisions of the invaders (30,000 men) during the process.

(Reports received by the Associated Press from Europe Sunday night said that Adolf Hitler's troops, in a move linked with the outbreak of war in the Pacific, were girding for offensives intended to take both Moscow and Leningrad and recapture Rostov "at any price" within two weeks.)

The Moscow radio said the Germans were beaten bloodily north of the capital (perhaps in the Klin or Dmitrov areas) and in the Kalinin sector, 95 miles to the northwest on the ice-bound Upper Volga. A village was reported recaptured in the Kalinin combat.

Russians acknowledged the continuance of heavy German pressure in the Tula zone south of Moscow.

German war dispatches implied that the intense cold had virtually paralyzed both armies on the central front. Local successes were claimed in the Donets basin.

75 Mile Gain

Kuibyshev dispatches declared the Russians had advanced from 50 to 75 miles in the three-week-old Rostov-Mariupol counter-offensive. Cossack cavalrymen were said to be slashing down Germans seeking to escape across the Mius river near Taganrog while Red army planes bombed their clogged routes of retreat.

The Soviet information bureau declared Russian air squadrons alone had accounted for 82 German planes, 143 tanks and 2,600 trucks and killed more than 8,000 men in these operations.

An indication that some of the Russian garrison which vacated the Hango naval base last week might have run the gantlet of German-Finnish mines and guns in the Gulf of Finland came from the Finnish high command.

"Between Seivasto and Ino," said a Helsinki communique, "our coast ...

Captive Mine Workers Get Union Shop

NEW YORK (AP) — The United Mine Workers of America (CIO) have reached an objective sought for more than 40 years — a union shop for miners in the major steel companies' captive coal pits. An arbitration board appointed by President Roosevelt to settle the thorny union shop issue — source of three recent strikes in the defense-vital captive mines — last night returned a 2 to 1 decision awarding the union its demand.

Decision Assailed

Benjamin F. Fairless, president of the U. S. Steel Corporation, returned the minority opinion, in which he assailed the board's decision as further imposing an "unlimited labor monopoly" upon the industry.

Dr. John R. Steelman, on leave as director of the U. S. Conciliation Service to serve on the Board, and John L. Lewis, union president, concurred in the majority agreement.

Lewis limited his comment to this statement: "I feel that the award justifies the position assumed by the United Mine Workers of America in regard to this conference."

As a result of the decision, these eight companies, having previously committed themselves to follow the Board's decision, will sign the Appalachain wage agreement, the standard for the country-wide bituminous coal industry.

By signing, the companies will grant the union shop, the only issue involved in the dispute. In separate stipulations with the union they already had granted wages and other conditions provided by the Appalachian agreement.

Union Shop Defined

Under the union shop, a miner must become a member of the union after he has been employed. Dr. Steelman said the issue was not, as Fairless referred to it, a "closed shop" in which only union members could be employed.

The issue, he said, was that of a "union shop agreement with an open union."

Companies affected by the award ...

Congress Backs President's Request For War With Japs With Near Unanimous Vo[te]

General Text Of FDR's Speech Today to Congress

(The text of President Roosevelt's war message to Congress follows:)

To the Congress of the United States:

Yesterday, Dec. 7, 1941, a date which will live in infamy, the United States of America was suddenly and deliberately attacked by naval and air forces of the Empire of Japan.

The United States was at peace with that nation and at the solicitation of Japan, was still in conversation with its government and its Emperor, looking toward the maintenance of peace in the Pacific.

War Not Mentioned

Indeed, one hour after Japanese air squadrons had commenced bombing in Oahu, the Japanese ambassador to the United States and his colleague, delivered to the Secretary of State, a formal reply to a recent American message. While this reply stated that it seemed useless to continue the existing diplomatic negotiations, it contained no threat or hint of war or armed attack.

It will be recorded that the distance of Hawaii from Japan makes it obvious that the attack was deliberately planned many days, or even weeks ago. During the intervening time the Japanese government has deliberately to deceive the United States by false statements and expressions of hope for continued peace.

American Loss Heavy

The attack yesterday on the Hawaiian island has caused severe damage to American naval and military forces. Very many American lives have been lost. In addition American ships have been reported torpedoed on the high seas between San Francisco and Honolulu.

Yesterday the Japanese government also launched an attack on Malaya.

Last night Japanese forces attacked Hong Kong.

Last night Japanese forces attacked Guam.

Last night Japanese forces attacked the Philippine Islands.

Last night the Japanese attacked Wake Island.

This morning the Japanese attacked Midway Island.

Japan has therefore, undertaken a surprise offensive extending throughout the Pacific area. The facts of yesterday speak for themselves. The people of the United States have already formed their opinions and well understand the implications to the very life and safety of our nation.

As commander in chief of the Army and Navy, I have directed that all measures be taken for our defense.

Victory Assured

Always will we remember the character of the onslaught against us.

No matter how long it may take us to overcome this premediated invasion, the American people in their righteous might, will win ...

WASHINGTON (AP) — The United States through its Congress, declared war today on Japan. Overwhelmingly and with the greatest unity shown in manany a day on capital hill, the Senate and the House backed up President Roosevelt's request for war declaration with unprecedented speed.

The Senate vote first to be recorded, was 82-0. The House vote was 388-1. The single adverse House vote was that of Miss Jeannette Rankin, Democratic congressman from Montana who was among the few who voted against the 1917 declaration of war on Germany.

(By the Associated Press)

The White House acknowledged today a bloody ... 3,000 killed and wounded in the Japanese attack on Honolulu as the battle of Hawaii continued and Imperial headquarters claimed smashing naval and air victories over the United States.

Great Britain formally declared war on Japan ... mighty forces of the United States fleet were reported ... ing the waters of the Pacific to seek battle with Jap warships.

Hawaii Damage Gre[at]

A White House stateme[nt ac]knowledged serious damage [to Am]erican forces in Hawaii b[ut con]siderably less than the losses which the Japanese ... they had inflicted.

The White House said Ja[panese] attacks had resulted in th[e cap]sizing of an old battleship, ... as the Japanese claim two ... ships had been sunk and r... the loss of a destroyer, dam... other vessels and destructio[n of a] relatively large number of ...

In London the House of [Com]mons cheered as Prime M[inister] Churchill fulfilling his pledg[e a] month ago, invoked war ... the Tokyo government.

The Netherlands East ... was the first government ... clare war on Japan. A... joined other members of th[e Brit]ish Empire in a declarat[ion of] war. In Havana the cabine[t asked] Cuba's Congress today to ... war.

Honolulu Assaulted

One or more Japanese ... carriers presumably escor[ted by] strong naval formations, w[ere re]ported to have engaged ... opening attack against Ho[nolulu].

This afternoon Japanese ... ers renewed attacks on th[e Phil]ippines, raiding the big U. S. encampment at Fort Stots... and nearby Clark field. Nu... buildings were set afire a... army's telephone communi[cations] to Manila were cut. Thre[e Jap]anese planes were reporte[d shot] down in the attacks.

In the Far East a Britis[h com]munique said Japanese ai... ers killed 63 persons and w... 133 today in a violent ass[ault on] Singapore, but that Ja[panese] troops were being "mopped ... an attempted land invas[ion of] Malaya from the north.

28-35 Years Availabl[e]

No Congressional actio[n] needed to make available ... lective service men in the ... year old bracket. The ...

Nazi Spokesman Calls President Father of War

BERLIN (AP) — A Wilhelmstrasse spokesman said today the course of the entire world would rest upon President Roosevelt, whom he called "the father of war," as he commented on the Far Eastern war.

The spokesman gave his comment in the daily press conference without waiting for questions from foreign correspondents.

He said he was not authorized to expound on the international angle as to who was the aggressor. However, he stated: "But from my commentary there should be little doubt about that."

As seen from a historical point of view, he asserted, it was unimportant whether war would be declared between Germany and the United States as a result of Far Eastern events.

Surprise Cited

The commentary Dienst Aus Deutschland, which has close connections with the foreign office, said today in a special issue that the American people and President Roosevelt may be assumed to be the only persons surprised at the expansion of war to the Far East.

The service said it could be assumed undoubtedly that Tokyo kept Berlin and Rome informed of all phases and therefore informed quarters were less surprised "than the German public.

The German government declared today President Roosevelt "finally has reached his aim by setting afire the Far East," but left unsaid what Germany's role would be in the new war involving her Japanese axis partner.

If the United States is considered the "attacked," it would suggest implications or Article Three of the axis accord which states that Germany, Japan and Italy "undertake to assist one another with all political, economic and military means" if one of the three signatories were attacked by a power not involved in the European or Asiatic struggles when the agreement was signed on Sept. 27, 1940.

West Coast Goes Into Fast Action

SAN FRANCISCO (AP) — Along the thousands of miles of American coastline that look out across the Pacific toward belligerent Japan, soldier, sailor and civilian alike today learned the meaning of war.

From Alaska to the Panama Canal hundreds of emergency measures were put into effect, from a few minutes to a few hours after Japan's fierce and sudden onslaught at Honolulu.

In the populous cities of the western seaboard, the first line of defense in event of an attack on continental United States, military and civilian agencies labored throughout the night to place the far west on an efficient war footing.

Recall of week-ending soldiers, sailors and marines to their posts was among the first orders. Police stopped them on the streets. Radios blared the orders. Taxicabs carried the men free.

Military posts were barred to civilians. Blackouts were ordered in Alaska and Panama and at the big airplane repair depot at Sacramento.

At San Diego an anti-submarine net was spread across the entrance to the huge fleet base. Puget Sound Navy yard warned that any airplane flying over it would be fired upon.

Jap Chute Troops Land in Philippines

NEW YORK (AP) — Royal Arch Gunnison, in a broadcast to WOR-Mutual from Manila, reported today that Japanese parachute troops had been landed in the Philippines.

Introduction

WHILE SMALLER IN SCALE, the American military aviation presence in Northern Ireland during the Second World War was almost as extensive in scope as in the remainder of the United Kingdom. It was here in January 1942 that US ground troops initially arrived in the UK. The first to disembark landed in Londonderry some hours before others stepped ashore in Belfast. They had travelled in the same convoy, NA1, of two British merchant ships and two Royal Navy escort vessels. A month later, work to construct a number of United States Army Air Forces' air depots and airfields throughout Great Britain and Northern Ireland commenced on the eastern shore of Lough Neagh at Langford Lodge, ancestral home of the Pakenham family. This was a remarkable historical irony for it was in January 1815, during the war between the USA and the UK, that British troops commanded by a distinguished member of the family, General Edward Pakenham, had been defeated at New Orleans by American troops commanded by Major General Andrew Jackson, the son of Ulster-Scots emigrants from Co Antrim.

What follows is a succinct account of the military aviation activities that took place at Langford Lodge as well as numerous other airfields and installations in Northern Ireland used by personnel and aircraft of the United States Army Air Forces, United States Naval Air Service and Lockheed Overseas Corporation. The story actually begins well before the USA officially entered the war.

In September 1939, most citizens of the United States of America had no desire to become involved in the Second World War.

2

Nevertheless, long before the country officially took up arms as a consequence of the surprise Japanese attack on Pearl Harbor on 7 December 1941 and Germany's declaration of war on the USA four days later, growing numbers of Americans were effectively supporting the United Kingdom and its allies.

From the outbreak of hostilities in September 1939, the US Government maintained an increasingly watchful attitude towards events in Europe and in 1940 began to send military observers to the UK. Among them was Major General James E Chaney, a veteran airman of the United States Army Air Corps. In December 1940, having formed the opinion that the Luftwaffe was overrated and that the UK would not be defeated, he submitted a report to the US War Department. This resulted, during the first three months of 1941, in secret discussions between US and UK armed forces representatives to determine the best methods of acting jointly in the event of US entry into the war, with the emphasis on defeating Germany first and, if necessary, Japan second. A role for Northern Ireland was envisaged from an early stage.

Major General James E Chaney

Also in December 1940, President Roosevelt began to formulate the Lend-Lease Act which came into effect in March 1941 and authorised him to sell, transfer title to or to otherwise dispose of military supplies or any other defence materials for which Congress appropriated funds, to 'the Government of any country whose defence the President deems vital to the defence of the United States.' Subsequent agreements between the American and British governments resulted in the creation of several military installations in the UK which were to be placed at the disposal of the USA in the event of war. They included a flying boat base on Lough Erne at Ely Lodge and Killadeas, construction of which was begun during the summer of 1941, by local employees working for US contractors with and under the supervision of American engineers and technicians. Commissioned by the US Navy early in 1942, in the event it was not used by them but was transferred to the Royal Air Force.

Killadeas

Meanwhile, in May 1941 a Special US Army Observer Group was activated in London with Chaney as its head, the purpose of which was to co-ordinate with British forces all details relative to the reception, accommodation and activities of US forces sent to the UK in the event of war. Losing no time, Chaney and his staff began to examine potential sites for Army and Army Air Corps (renamed Army Air Forces in 1941) installations in the UK and to make tentative arrangements. By September 1941, he and his associates were recommending the eventual establishment of a USAAF 'Interceptor Command' in Northern Ireland as well as the urgent development of an air depot at Langford Lodge. The immediate purpose of the latter would be to provide for maintenance and repair of increasing numbers of American aircraft then being supplied to and operated by British forces and ultimately of American aircraft operated by that country's own military forces.

Langford Lodge pre-war

4

1 Volunteer pilots

Badge of No. 133 (Eagle) Squadron

Roland 'Bud' Wolfe

Ironically, by then, despite breaking US laws and incurring the ire of the US Government, hundreds of Americans had volunteered to fly with the RAF and Royal Canadian Air Force. Many became bomber crew but around 250 were trained as fighter pilots and three RAF 'Eagle' Squadrons were formed in England to accommodate many of them. The first, No. 71, formed in September 1940, followed by No. 121 in May 1941 and No. 133 in August 1941. On 8 October 1941, when it was just commencing the process of converting from Hurricanes to Spitfires, No. 133 Squadron was transferred to RAF Eglinton, becoming the first squadron to use this new airfield as a base. Tragically, its re-deployment began inauspiciously, four pilots being killed en route when their Hurricanes crashed on the Isle of Man during bad weather. One of them, Andy Mamedoff from Connecticut, was a Battle of Britain veteran. Before the month was out, two more of the Squadron's pilots, one a Canadian, were to die as a result of flying accidents, at Rasharkin in Co Antrim and Eglinton itself. The Squadron's role was to defend the city of Londonderry and its naval base and to escort convoys in coastal waters. However, tragedies apart, its three-month sojourn at Eglinton was comparatively uneventful, except for one pilot's remarkable experience. On 1 December 1941, Pilot Officer Roland 'Bud' Wolfe, a Nebraskan, was flying a convoy escort mission when the engine of his Spitfire developed a coolant leak, overheated and he was obliged to bale out over Co Donegal. Apprehended by the Eire authorities for a breach of the country's neutrality, he was interned in the Curragh in Co Kildare. A fortnight later, by subterfuge, he managed to walk out of the camp gates and return to Eglinton, only to be sent back by Air Ministry authority for conduct unbecoming an officer! In 1943, he was officially released, joined the USAAF in England, survived the war, two subsequent conflicts in Korea and Vietnam and died peacefully in 1994.

Not all American volunteer fighter pilots in the RAF flew with the 'Eagle' Squadrons. A grave in the Churchyard of Christ Church,

Flight Sergeant
William B Fry

Limavady bears silent testimony 5
to that. It contains the remains
of Flight Sergeant William B Fry
from Texas who was a member
of No. 504 Squadron, RAF, based
at Ballyhalbert in Co Down.
He was killed when his Spitfire
crashed near Dungiven when
participating in a joint military
exercise involving British and
American ground forces and
aircraft on 26 September 1942.

2 Eighth Air Force Composite Command

Eighth Air Force
shoulder sleeve insignia

With US entry into the war, the tentative plans regarding Northern
Ireland envisaged by Chaney and others during 1941 were endorsed
and expanded in scope to provide for essential European Theatre
operational training of fighter and bomber crews arriving fresh
from the USA and the accommodation of transport units. The basic
aim was to conserve airfields in England for combat units and
it was envisaged that 17 airfields would be required in Northern
Ireland. In July 1942, these plans appeared to get off to a good start
with the formation of the Eighth Air Force Composite Command
in the USA to oversee all of this activity, including responsibility
for the fighter defence of Northern Ireland. Like many wartime
plans, however, they were only partially realised for various reasons,
primarily because of the Allied decision to invade French North-
West Africa, first mooted in August 1941 but serious planning for
which did not begin until mid-1942. In the event, 13 airfields did
come to be used by the USAAF but only six were handed over to
become Army Air Force stations. They were Langford Lodge,
Toome, Greencastle, Cluntoe, Maghaberry and Mullaghmore.

6

At the remaining seven the US presence was in a 'lodger' capacity and the RAF retained control of them, i.e. Ballykelly, Eglinton, Maydown, Long Kesh, Nutts Corner, Sandy Bay and Sydenham.

In August 1942, an advance party of 10 officers of the Eighth Air Force Composite Command arrived at RAF Long Kesh where quarters were made available to accommodate them and the main party of around 400 officers and enlisted men which followed in mid-September, until more permanent accommodation was provided at Kircassock House, the former summer residence near Magheralin in Co Down of the hat-making Christie-Miller family. Two months later, around 80 buildings comprising barrack huts, mess halls, sick quarters, administrative offices, fire station and sewage disposal works which had been constructed in the grounds of Kircassock House were occupied to become the Command's HQ (AAF Station 231, code-name 'Nyack') while the House itself became the Officers' Club.

Command personnel arrived expecting to do immediate business but the decision to invade North-West Africa seriously slowed the

Kircassock House

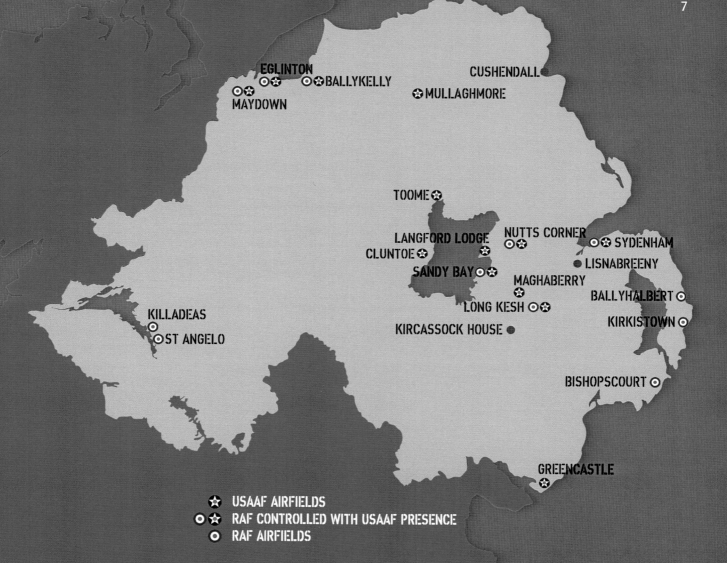

EGLINTON ⊙⊙✪ ⊙✪BALLYKELLY   CUSHENDALL

MAYDOWN   ✪MULLAGHMORE

TOOME✪

LANGFORD LODGE   NUTTS CORNER

CLUNTOE✪   ✪ ⊙✪ ⊙⊙✪SYDENHAM

SANDY BAY⊙✪   ⬤LISNABREENY

MAGHABERRY✪

KILLADEAS⊙   LONG KESH⊙⊙   BALLYHALBERT⊙

⊙ST ANGELO   KIRKISTOWN⊙

KIRCASSOCK HOUSE⬤

BISHOPSCOURT⊙

GREENCASTLE✪

✪   USAAF AIRFIELDS
⊙✪   RAF CONTROLLED WITH USAAF PRESENCE
⊙   RAF AIRFIELDS

build-up of the Eighth Air Force in the UK. This left them with comparatively little to do for months apart from dealing with administrative matters common to Army Air Forces stations generally such as military discipline, morale, general housekeeping, relations with the local civilian population and General Courts Martial.

8

3 Interceptor Command

The 'Interceptor Command' (*Fighter Command* in RAF terminology) is a good example of how proposals came to be curtailed. Initially, it was envisaged that USAAF day and night fighters would be based at the airfields of Ballyhalbert, Kirkistown, Eglinton, Maydown and St Angelo to relieve RAF Fighter Command of responsibility for the air defence of Northern Ireland. On 13 July 1942, pilots and ground staff of the three squadrons of the 52nd Fighter Group of the Eighth Air Force disembarked from a ship at Larne Harbour and made their way to Eglinton and Maydown, to which 35 British Spitfires had already been delivered for their use. By 15 July, the total delivered had reached 46, in what was an early example of Reverse Lend-Lease. However, the Group's time in Northern Ireland was comparatively short; by 13 September all aircrew had been transferred to England with their Spitfires, a process which began on 25 August upon their assignment to the Twelfth Air Force in North-West Africa. Being completely new to Spitfires, the Group's pilots spent much of their time at Eglinton and Maydown becoming familiar with the type, participating in exercises of various kinds and working up to operational readiness by carrying out a small number of practice scrambles and defensive patrols. Tragically, this was not without human cost, 2nd Lieutenant Earl Sharpe of the Group's 4th Fighter Squadron, also a Texan, being killed when his Spitfire crashed near Portrush on 11 August.

Badge of 82nd Fighter Group

At the beginning of October, their place at Eglinton and Maydown was taken by personnel of the three squadrons of the 82nd Fighter Group. However, it was 13 November before their Lockheed P-38 fighters began to be delivered from the air depot at Speke airport, Liverpool, most of the intervening time being devoted to drill and rest although some of the Group's pilots were given opportunities to fly Spitfires that were based at Eglinton with a resident RAF squadron. On 16 December 1942, the 82nd Fighter Group began to leave for England, a process which involved more than 40 P-38s and lasted until the beginning of January 1943. Sadly, the process was marked by tragedy when, on 16 December, a P-38 on delivery

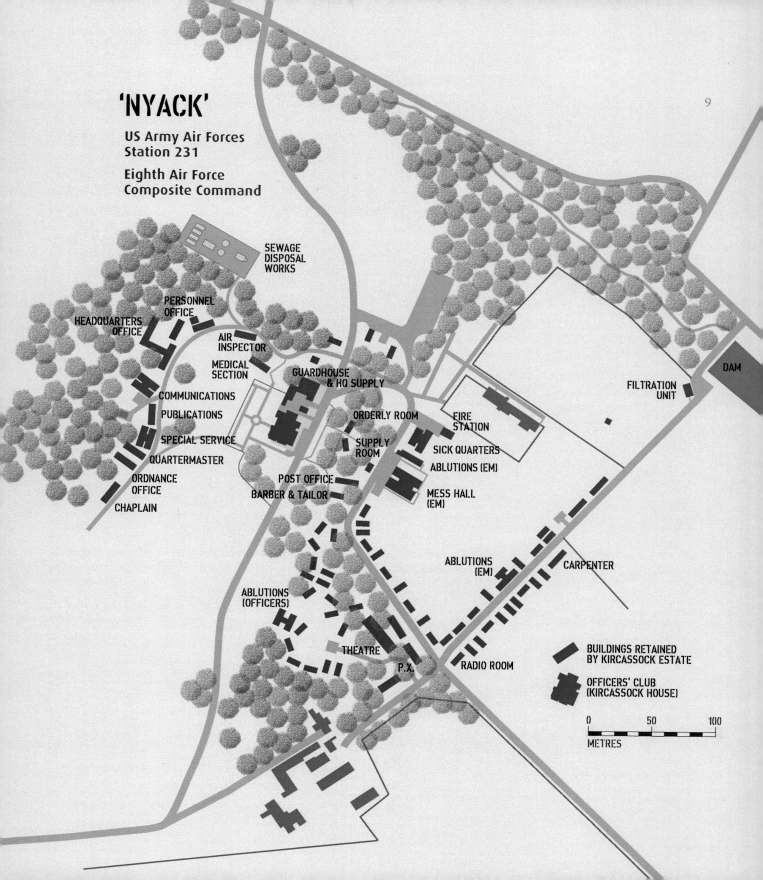

'NYACK'

US Army Air Forces
Station 231

Eighth Air Force
Composite Command

SEWAGE
DISPOSAL
WORKS

PERSONNEL
OFFICE

HEADQUARTERS
OFFICE

AIR
INSPECTOR

MEDICAL
SECTION

GUARDHOUSE
& HQ SUPPLY

COMMUNICATIONS

PUBLICATIONS

ORDERLY ROOM

SPECIAL SERVICE

SUPPLY
ROOM

FIRE
STATION

QUARTERMASTER

SICK QUARTERS

ORDNANCE
OFFICE

POST OFFICE

ABLUTIONS (EM)

BARBER & TAILOR

MESS HALL
(EM)

CHAPLAIN

DAM

FILTRATION
UNIT

ABLUTIONS
(EM)

CARPENTER

ABLUTIONS
(OFFICERS)

THEATRE

P.X.

RADIO ROOM

BUILDINGS RETAINED
BY KIRCASSOCK ESTATE

OFFICERS' CLUB
(KIRCASSOCK HOUSE)

0   50   100

METRES

9

Maydown, August 1942

from Langford Lodge to Eglinton for subsequent flight to England, dived into the runway at Langford Lodge at high speed, instantly killing the pilot, 21-year-old 2nd Lieutenant Scott K Giles, from Kansas. There were indications he had decided to put on a 'bit of a show' on departure from Langford Lodge but lost control when looping the aircraft. Like the 52nd Fighter Group, the 82nd Fighter Group went to North-West Africa, marking the end of plans for an 'Interceptor Command'.

4 Langford Lodge

Langford Lodge Air Depot, which was officially designated No. 3 Base Air Depot in September 1943, was the largest single USAAF airfield to be developed in Northern Ireland. It was one of three base air depots in the UK but, unlike the others at Burtonwood and Warton in Lancashire, it was operated by the civilian Lockheed Overseas Corporation (LOC) on behalf of and under the supervision of the Eighth Air Force Service Command until a unique contract between both organisations was terminated by the USAAF in May 1944. Collectively, these air depots provided complete logistical support to four American air forces which operated in the European and Mediterranean/North African Theatres of War – the Eighth, Ninth, Twelfth and Fifteenth Air Forces. LOC was a logical choice to operate the depot, having been established at Liverpool in February 1939 by the California-based Lockheed Aircraft Corporation to assemble American aircraft being supplied to the RAF on foot of orders which the British Purchasing Commission had begun to place in 1938. Moreover, there is evidence that in 1941 the company

No.3 Base Air Depot plaque

Langford Lodge Air Depot, September 1943

12

had established facilities in a hangar at Sydenham airfield to prepare Boston aircraft for the RAF although it is questionable whether that particular work actually took place.

Construction of the Langford Lodge depot began in February 1942, on land which had been acquired a year earlier by the UK Ministry of Aircraft Production for use as a small satellite landing ground for the storage of aircraft on behalf of No. 23 Maintenance Unit based nearby at RAF Aldergrove. Plans for the depot as drawn up by the ministry included provision for the erection of barrack huts on five distinct living sites with integral communal facilities, numerous hangars, workshops, warehouses and construction of three hard-surfaced runways, albeit only two of the runways were actually built. In July 1942 a hospital building was constructed but it was mid-September before it became possible for the first patients to be admitted because delivery of medical equipment and supplies was delayed due to the war. It was a brick-built structure, in the form of an 'H', comprising offices, reception rooms, dispensary, X-Ray room, pharmacy, dental clinic, laboratories, operating theatre, surgical ward, respiratory ward, general ward, isolation wards, kitchen and stores. Records indicate that the initial capacity was 55 beds but by the last year of the war this had been reduced to 34. Early in the intervening period it was proposed to increase the capacity to 150 beds by making use of prefabricated timber huts but there is no evidence that this was ever put into effect. From 1942 until mid-1944 during which period LOC managed Langford Air Depot, the hospital was equipped to perform all types of surgery and medical treatment and was considered to be one of the most modern installations in Northern Ireland. Doctors, nurses and medical staff were Americans contracted by LOC. Upon the assumption of control by the USAAF in June 1944 following termination of the contract with LOC, considerable quantities of medical equipment and supplies were removed, on the basis that the US Army hospital at Waringfield, Moira, was equipped and able to perform the more serious elective surgeries and treatment, hence the reduction to 34-bed capacity. By January 1945 however, Waringfield had closed and it was found necessary to requisition sufficient equipment and supplies to enable the Langford Lodge

Langford Lodge hospital

Hospital doctors, dentists and nursing personnel

facility to deal with emergency and minor types of elective surgery, some of the equipment being manufactured on site by USAAF engineers. To complement medical staff at Langford Lodge, a platoon of the 55th US Field Hospital was assigned to the base. The main contractor appointed to construct the depot was Sir Lindsay Parkinson. Upon request, the Great Northern Railway built two and a half miles

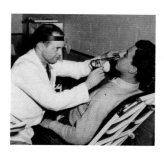
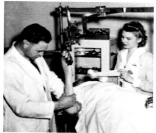

of single-line rail track to link the depot with the main railway network at Crumlin which was brought into operation in May 1942. Unfortunately, despite being accorded absolute priority over all other building work in Northern Ireland and planned to be completed within six months, construction of the air depot fell behind schedule, with the result that when American technicians began to arrive in June 1942, expecting to begin the work for which they had been contracted, the airfield was not in a fit state to receive aircraft and some of the men were handed picks and shovels to assist with building work. Others were temporarily detached to Great Britain to help service and maintain aircraft arriving as part of the build-up of USAAF military strength there.

14

MECHANICS WANTED

FOR EXCITING SERVICE OVERSEAS AS WARPLANE REPAIR MEN

If you have had two years experience as a mechanic—or the equivalent in practical shop training—here's how you can service America. Learn a trade with a great future and earn premium pay.

Lockheed Overseas Corporation needs men to serve overseas in non-combat areas as aviation mechanics.

No aviation experience needed; You will be paid during the 8 weeks training. Then upon satisfactory completion of the course your pay is increased to overseas rates.

CLASSES NOW STARTING

You can start at Lockheed's Memphis, Tenn., School now. We pay Transportation from your home to Memphis, so apply immediately. You can serve your country by keeping her warplanes flying.

If you are in 1-A or under 18, or if you are engaged at your highest skill and in an essential activity you will not be considered. Apply in person at the

U. S. EMPLOYMENT SERVICE
of THE WAR MANPOWER COMMISSION
AT
40 STEUBEN ST.   ALBANY, N. Y.

USA newspaper advertisement, July 1943

During the USAAF/LOC contract period up to May 1944, around 4000 US civilians, men and women, were brought from the USA to work for LOC at Langford Lodge. Recruited from some of the major US aircraft and defence establishments, they were among the most highly skilled technicians in the world and their collective talents enabled virtually every aspect of aircraft servicing, engineering and assembly work to be accomplished, what the Americans referred to as fourth echelon. They lived in centrally-heated huts in one or other of four of the living sites, a fifth being reserved for US Army and Army Air Forces personnel. Over the same period, the LOC American civilian personnel were complemented by more or less similar numbers of local civilians recruited to perform a variety of jobs, including office clerks, telephonists, building labourers, canteen staff and truck drivers, for example. They commuted to work on a daily basis, by public rail or road transport or in vehicles sent out by LOC to collect them. Some of the American technicians were on short-term contracts, others were there for the duration of the war. Members of the US military formed a third category, albeit in the period up to June 1944 when the contract with LOC ended, the number in that group rarely exceeded 1500. On 1 January 1944, a 'snapshot' survey revealed a total of 6900 on the base – 2913 local civilian employees, 2883 Lockheed personnel including female hospital nursing staff and 1104 US military. Little wonder the place was sometimes referred to as 'Lockheed city'.

Local civilian employees arrive for work

Aircraft instrument technician Charles Stover was one of the first Americans to arrive at Langford Lodge in July 1942

LOCKHEED OVERSEAS CORPORATION
2400 WEST ALAMEDA STREET
BURBANK, CALIFORNIA

NAME	DATE	TIME		EARNINGS					DED
		REG.	O.T.	REG.	O.T.	BONUS	GROSS	F.O.A.	S.U.I.	
Charles H. Stover	6-30-42			142.50			142.50	1.43	.71	

LOC. 324 PRINTED IN U.S.A

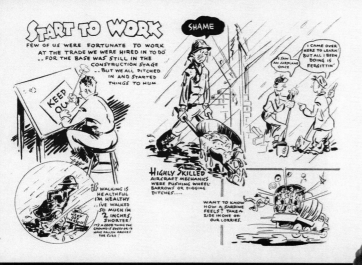

Many local women were employed in a variety of jobs on the base

16

Work practices and rules booklet
issued to LOC technicians

Lockheed Overseas Corporation
Arm Badge

The processing of USAAF aircraft at the depot began on 27 October 1942, when urgent modification work commenced on B-24 Liberator bombers of the 44th Bomb Group, Eighth Air Force, the so-called Flying Eightballs. Based in Norfolk, England, as a constituent of Eighth Air Force Bomber Command, they had begun to arrive in the UK from late September and throughout October and November. Simultaneously, growing numbers of Douglas C-47 transport aircraft began to arrive, some to undergo repairs and some to be modified for use by the Twelfth Air Force in North Africa. On Armistice Day, 11 November 1942, aircraft reassembly work commenced with the arrival of the first of many P-38 Lockheed Lightning fighters which were brought by road from Belfast, to which large numbers would eventually be shipped from the USA as deck cargo. For Lockheed's technicians, many of whom had previously been building these aircraft in California, sight of them was a welcome boost to morale.

The work done to a large proportion of P-38s in succeeding weeks involved the installation of special air filters, betraying their intended use in North Africa. As the year drew to a close, some of the 82nd Fighter Group's P-38s were flown in from Eglinton, to which they had originally been flown from Liverpool or Langford Lodge itself in some cases. Towards the end of November, assembly work commenced on considerable numbers of yet another aircraft type, the Brewster Bermuda dive-bomber which in 1940 had been selected by the British Purchasing Commission for the RAF but proved unsuited to the role.

Bermudas at
Langford Lodge

As originally conceived, it was anticipated that most of the reassembly and maintenance work to be carried out at Langford Lodge would involve American aircraft in RAF service and, by January 1942, a few B-24 Liberators and B-17 Fortresses of RAF Coastal Command were undergoing repairs. Inevitably though, between November 1942 and April 1944, almost all the aircraft that passed through the depot were of virtually every type used by the American Eighth, Ninth, Twelfth and Fifteenth Air Forces. During that period, work of a reassembly, modification, repair, major overhaul or salvage nature was carried out on 3300 aircraft and a further 11,000 were serviced. Gradually though, two types came to predominate in the aircraft modification programme: P-38 Lightnings and B-17 Flying Fortresses. Moreover, it wasn't just aircraft. Up to January 1944, 555 aircraft engines were stripped down and rebuilt. Between July 1943 and April 1944, 274,000 spark plugs were refurbished while 11,500 propellers were cleaned, adjusted or further overhauled. Significantly, the spark plug production lines were staffed almost exclusively by locally recruited women.

Many local women were employed in a variety of jobs on the base

During the first half of 1943, engineering work rapidly increased and in June, the depot was given technical responsibility for the modification of all aircraft in the European Theatre of Operations. Instructions were issued by Service Command to increase the facilities required and because hangar and storage accommodation was limited, the RAF airfield at Greencastle was taken over as a

Greencastle airfield in 1943

satellite depot. Unfortunately, it was soon realised that the dispersed nature of the hangar layout there compared to Langford Lodge constrained production. However, despite the proximity to sea air, it was considered more suitable for aircraft storage and 100 new hard standings were constructed for that purpose.

Whereas there was a great deal of commonality in the type of work carried out at all the base air depots, at least three projects were initiated at Langford Lodge. In December 1942, the first of at least five mobile repair units to be assembled and fitted out was driven to England to facilitate the field repair of USAAF aircraft damaged as a result of forced landings away from their parent air bases. Each unit consisted of two trailer vans drawn by a single motor tractor unit. One van was equipped with compressed air tools, compressors, lathes, drill presses and other essential equipment while the second van provided sleeping quarters and kitchen. During the first few months of field use, LOC men on detached service made up most of the crew, complemented by USAAF mechanics. In June 1943, there occurred a logical development of the original concept when a Waco CG4-A glider was adapted for aircraft service and repair work. Similarly equipped to the mobile repair units in conformity with load limits, it was named *Mechanikite* and air-towed to England for trials at a P-47 Thunderbolt fighter base.

Mobile Repair Units prepare to leave for England

A third project, involving 12,000 man-hours of work by the Engineering Design department, was urgently commenced at Langford lodge in February 1944. To a design by George McCutcheon, the forward fuselage of a single-seat P-38 fighter was re-modelled by removing the nose armament and using the enlarged space to incorporate a Norden bombsight, armour plate and seat for a bomb aimer to create what came to be known as the *Droop Snoot* Lightning. This enabled it to be used as a lead aircraft to mark targets for mass formation bombing by conventional P-38s carrying bombs at twice the speed of heavy bombers. The project was completed by USAAF engineers in August 1944 after the contract with LOC had ended, by which time 26 Droop Snoots had been produced at Langford Lodge, plus around 100 kits to permit additional P-38s to be built elsewhere. It is known that some were produced in Britain and others in India.

Droop Snoot nose mock-up and production line

5 Storage and Experimental Station

In June 1944, a new chapter in Langford Lodge's history began when it was re-designated a Storage and Experimental Station, under the complete control of Eighth Air Force Service Command. Termination of the contract with LOC reflected no major shortcomings on the company's part; rather, the combined capacities of the depots in Britain had increased to the point where they were capable of carrying most of the logistical burden. As a result, Langford Lodge was enabled to devote a much greater proportion of time to research and development. To that end, some of the highly qualified and experienced LOC personnel were retained to be employed as US civil servants in the newly established Modification & Technical Control Section which had an establishment of 17 USAAF officers, 102 enlisted men, 65 civil service technicians and 34 local civilian employees. Regarded by these personnel as the 'nerve centre' of the Station, its work was highly specialised and included responsibility for developing maintenance standards as well as the technical development and control of aircraft in the European Theatre of Operations.

Irish personnel of the
Modification & Technical Control Section

Working alongside the technicians and USAAF engineers transferred from Burtonwood were local civilians John Abernethy and Bill Govan, experimental physicist/ spectroscopist and engineering draftsman, respectively.

Reference has previously been made to the *Droop Snoot* work; other novel projects undertaken under the auspices of the Modification and Technical Control Section included the modification of medium bombers to carry and dispense

IRISH PERSONNEL

Colonel Goddard at Langford Lodge

Hundreds of B-24 Liberator aircraft in storage at Langford Lodge, August 1944

'chaff' (strips of aluminium foil to confuse radar signals), adapting a P-51 Mustang fighter to carry reconnaissance cameras in the wings, a top priority main undercarriage emergency release modification for A-26 aircraft and another to install night photographic equipment in Mosquito aircraft, including racks for M46 photoflash 'bombs'. This last project, involving considerable numbers of Mosquitoes from the Eighth Air Force's 325th Photographic Wing commanded by Colonel Elliott Roosevelt, son of the President, was carried out under the oversight of the USAAF's Colonel George W Goddard whose contribution to the development of aerial reconnaissance throughout the Second World War and afterwards came to be regarded as outstanding.

As the war neared its end, war-weary aircraft were flown to Langford Lodge for storage or to be broken up and salvaged, to such an extent that in March 1945, four months before the base closed, the largest number of aircraft ever to be parked on the airfield and the extensive dispersal areas at one time was 572.

21

6   Socio-economic and cultural impact

The renewable contract drawn up between the Eighth Air Force and LOC and signed in May 1942 committed the US government to an expenditure of $30 million at Langford Lodge, at contemporary values. It was renewed at six-month intervals, in the course of which additional funds were made available. This enabled LOC to pay wages and salaries to locally recruited civilians several times the rate for comparable work in Northern Ireland. And American

Some of the children in an aircraft at the base

generosity didn't stop there. In the run-up to Christmas 1942, American civilian employees at Langford Lodge funded parties for 4000 local children and also contributed enough cash to a War Orphans Fund to create a trust fund to meet the welfare requirements of 17 children whose fathers had been killed as a result of Luftwaffe bombing raids on Belfast in the spring of 1941. Via the auspices of the Belfast Council for Social Welfare, they were brought to the base from time to time for treats and special events.

Some of the children with Lockheed heads of departments

In spite of the demands of war work, American personnel found time to relax, on and off the base. On site, a wide range of entertainment and recreational interests was catered for, including facilities for badminton, baseball, basketball, bowling and tennis as well as amateur photo laboratory, rifle range, library and radio broadcasting studio for the depot's *Nit Wit* Network. In December 1942, a 750-capacity cinema/theatre was opened, equipped with state-of-the-art 35mm film projection equipment which enabled the latest Hollywood releases to be screened. It was here that the Glenn Miller Band played to a capacity audience on 13 August 1944,

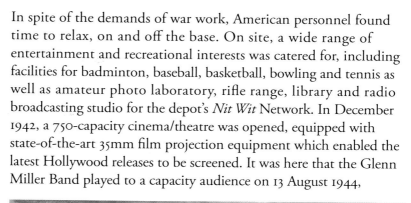

Baseball player at Langford Lodge

Bob Hope visiting the base hospital with Tony Romano and Jack Pepper

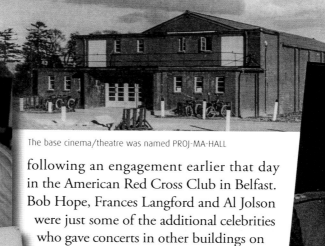

The base cinema/theatre was named PROJ-MA-HALL

following an engagement earlier that day in the American Red Cross Club in Belfast. Bob Hope, Frances Langford and Al Jolson were just some of the additional celebrities who gave concerts in other buildings on the base.

Glenn Millar at PROJ-MA-HALL

In the search for other forms of recreation and entertainment, Belfast and other towns were much frequented by LOC and Army Air Forces personnel, the American Red Cross Club, Plaza Ballroom and 400 Club in Chichester Street, Grand Central Hotel in Royal Avenue and Floral Hall at Bellevue being among the most popular attractions. So too, but at a domestic scale, were the homes of local families where homespun entertainment and hospitality was greatly appreciated and lasting friendships formed.

24

7 Aircraft deliveries

The delivery of thousands of aircraft from the USA to the USAAF in the UK was a huge and extensive operation. Heavy bomber and large transport aircraft were flown across the Atlantic by combat as well as ferrying crews while light bombers, fighters and small communications aircraft were transported by sea, either crated in the holds or partially disassembled and lashed to the decks of merchant ships or in aircraft carriers. Direct deliveries to Great Britain commenced in significant numbers in the summer of 1942 but the first direct deliveries to Langford Lodge came in November when P-38 Lightning fighters were off-loaded from a ship at Pollock Dock, Belfast. In succeeding months, P-47 Thunderbolts and P-51 Mustangs arrived by similar means but were off-loaded at the deep-water berth adjoining Sydenham airfield where LOC personnel on detachment from Langford Lodge re-assembled the aircraft by re-fitting tailplanes, fins and propellers that had been packed in crates. The aircraft were then flown to Langford Lodge where modification work was performed before they were test flown prior to onward flight to combat bases in England. No other airfield in the UK enjoyed such direct access to a deep-water berth.

P-47 Thunderbolts await unloading at the deep-water berth adjacent to Sydenham airfield

In the case of P-38s, a different procedure was followed. Ships carrying these larger, twin-engine fighters with the portions of wing outboard of the engines removed, were offloaded on the Co. Antrim side of the port from where they were initially towed by road on specially fabricated trailers to Langford Lodge where the wings and propellers were reunited with the airframes and modifications carried out before they were test flown. As the flow of P-38s increased, this particular method of towing proved too slow to cope so LOC engineers devised a special rig which enabled the aircraft to be towed on their own undercarriage wheels. All stevedoring work at the port was performed by George Heyn & Son and records indicate the company was responsible for offloading well over 1000 aircraft that were shipped to Belfast during the war.

The other location, one of four in the UK (Prestwick, Valley and St Mawgan were the others) for reception of the aircraft that were flown across the Atlantic was Nutts Corner. This airfield first came into use in the summer of 1941 as the base of RAF Coastal Command's 120 Squadron, the first to be equipped with American B-24

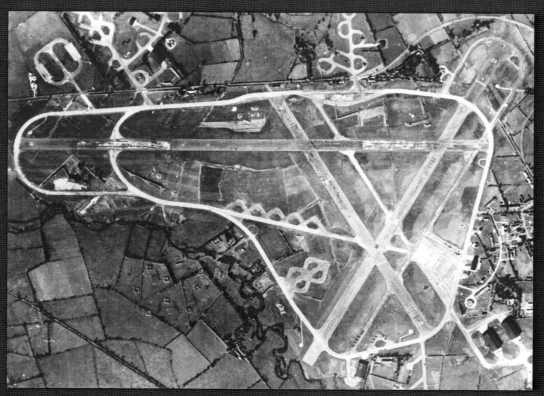

Nutts Corner in 1945

Liberator anti-submarine aircraft supplied under Lend-Lease. By mid-1942, in anticipation of a rapid build-up of the Eighth Air Force in the UK, the decision was taken to adapt it as a transatlantic reception centre, to which end work began to lengthen runways and increase aircraft parking spaces, construction of which continued well into 1944. In July 1943 the first arrivals were recorded, B-17 Flying Fortresses which flew in via Gander in Newfoundland. Gradually, they were followed by different types, with increasing intensity, July 1944 being a record breaking month when 372 aircraft arrived – 246 B-17s, 90 B-24s, 12 B-26s and 24 C-47s. The flights were rarely uneventful, whether for reasons of weather, navigational or technical difficulties. On 13 January 1944, for example, 24 bombers left Goose Bay, of which eight made it to Nutts Corner but eight landed at St Angelo, two at Sydenham and one each at Ballyhalbert and Cluntoe while a further two landed in Scotland, at Turnberry and Evanton. The remaining two crash-landed, one at Carrickfergus and the other in Loch Quoich in Scotland which resulted in the death of one of the crew. In other cases, flights ended even more tragically, to which reference will be made later.

Usually, the aircraft were initially collected at modification centres or departure airfields in the USA and were then flown in stages to the UK. Often, aircrew assigned to join combat Bomb Groups in England flew their own aircraft across while replacement aircraft were flown by the North Atlantic Wing of Air Transport Command's Operational Ferry Service, its pilots returning direct from Nutts Corner or one of the other ferry terminals in Britain, leaving the aircraft there to be flown to depots by crews from Transport or Ferrying Squadrons based in the UK. To facilitate the navigation of aircraft on delivery, there was a non-directional radio beacon two miles south west of Belleek at Derrynacross in Co. Fermanagh operated by the RAF (coded UU7) and two four-course radio ranges that were operated by the USAAF, one two miles east of Belleek at Magherameenagh (UU) and the other between Nutts Corner and Aldergrove (HU) which was associated with a fan marker at Langford Lodge.

A logistics operation of this kind depended on a range of support facilities, including accurate weather forecasting. In February 1944 the Americans established a mobile RAWIN (acronym for RADAR WINDS) Station at Nutts Corner which became invaluable to meteorologists in making forecasts. Similar facilities existed at St Mawgan in Cornwall and Stornoway in the Outer Hebrides. In simple terms a hydrogen-filled balloon carrying a radar target, radio and pressure sensor was released and tracked by radar or theodolite to determine wind speeds at various heights, readings being transmitted electronically to the ground station. All the while, although designated by the USAAF as AAF Station No. 235 within the European Wing of Air Transport Command, Nutts Corner remained under RAF Control.

9 Ferrying Squadrons

Within the UK the USAAF assumed entire responsibility for delivering military aircraft to its forces and those of the US Naval Air Service. In contrast, the British equivalent was the Air Transport Auxiliary (ATA) which consisted of volunteer civilian pilots, some of whom were ex-service and around 12 per cent of whom were women. Here too, the civilians included American volunteers, male and female, 25 being women, representing about 16 per cent of the ATA's complement of women pilots. One of the latter, Mary Nicholson from North Carolina, was the only American female pilot to be killed, on 22 May 1943 when the single-engine aircraft she was delivering lost a propeller and crashed in Worcestershire. The ATA had 14 Ferry Pilots Pools at airfields

Pilots of No. 8 Ferry Pilots Pool, Howard Trunnell seated at extreme left

George Clark with B-17 at Langford Lodge

throughout the UK, including No. 8 Ferry Pilots Pool at Sydenham where one of its 20 or so pilots was an American civilian, Howard Trunnell. In 1943 he and another American pilot, George Clark, were 'head-hunted' from the ATA by LOC to serve as test pilots at Langford Lodge, where Clark became Chief Test Pilot.

In 1942 initially, ferrying of aircraft and transporting of supplies were part of the overall function of Troop Carrier Groups based in England but in February 1943 a provisional Ferry and Transport Service was created, followed in April by the creation of the 27th Air Transport Group based at Hendon, north of London, with a detachment at Langford Lodge. Further refinement occurred during the autumn when Ferrying Squadrons began to be set up, including the 310th at Warton Base Air Depot in Lancashire, and two, the 311th and 312th together with the 321st Transport Squadron in November 1943 at Maghaberry airfield which was handed over by the RAF to become an Army Air Forces station. This airfield became the main UK base for USAAF Ferrying Squadrons until May 1944 when both were transferred to Langford Lodge (to which the 321st TS had been re-located in January), with detachments based at USAAF airfields in Britain, including Prestwick in Scotland and Grove in Berkshire. Also during this period, the airfield was employed by casualty evacuation aircraft of the Ninth Air Force to transport US military patients to and from the US 79th Station Hospital at Moira, nearby. Maghaberry's days as the main base for Ferrying and Transport Squadrons ended in 1944 and it was handed back to the RAF in June. By October 1944, Ferrying and Transport Squadrons were no longer based in Northern Ireland, aircraft being flown to and from Langford Lodge by pilots based in Britain or the few resident test pilots at the base itself.

Despite early plans that Northern Ireland would become the main centre of aircrew training in the UK, this scheme was slow to get under way and did not develop to the extent originally envisaged, being restricted to bomber crews. The organisation created for the specific purpose of training crews was known as a Combat Crew Replacement Center Group (CCRC) which consisted of two elements, a HQ & HQ Squadron and a Replacement & Training Squadron. In Northern Ireland, four CCRCs were activated on paper, the Third, Fourth, Fifth and Sixth, to make use of the airfields at Toome, Cluntoe, Greencastle and Mullaghmore respectively. Practically speaking, however, training did not commence until September 1943 when the Third CCRC at Toome began to use twin-engine B-26 Marauders and A-20 Havocs to instruct medium bomber crews. In November, the Fourth CCRC at Cluntoe

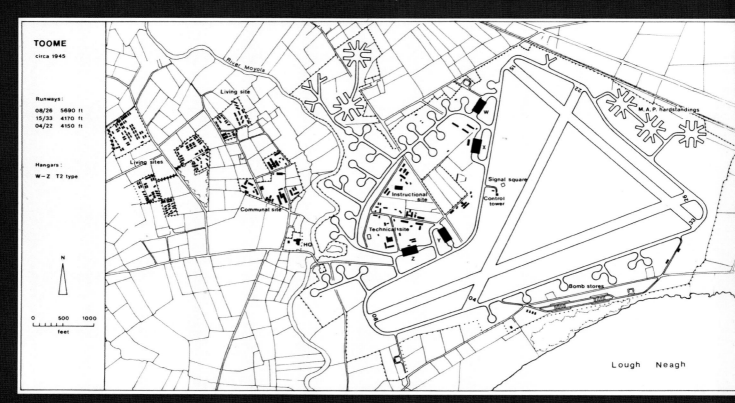

30

commenced the training of heavy bomber crews using B-17 Fortresses. In February 1944, in a nominal 'paper move', the Fourth was replaced by the Second CCRC which signalled a change of bomber type to B-24 Liberators, albeit the Replacement & Training Squadron of the Fourth CCRC transferred to Greencastle to operate with the Gunnery School which had opened there in December 1943. Early in 1944, in anticipation of the forthcoming landings in Europe and with a view to moving forces forward, the decision was taken to re-locate the Eighth Air Force Composite Command to England from where it continued to administer the bomber training programme throughout the UK until its disbandment in September 1944. At the same time, the Sixth CCRC which had not become operational, left Mullaghmore which was then occupied for a short time by paratroopers of the US 82nd Airborne Division, use being made of hangars to dry out parachutes which had been used in Italy. From then until Mullaghmore was handed back to the RAF in May 1944, opportunity was taken to use the airfield for the storage of aircraft to relieve pressure on Langford Lodge.

Ground-based gun turrets at Greencastle

Whereas the Fifth CCRC did not become fully operational, nevertheless Greencastle did play a vital role in the training of bomber crews, from the closing weeks of 1943 when the Gunnery School was established. Here CCRC gunnery training was concentrated, target drogue towing being provided by the Fourth Gunnery & Tow Target Flight of the Eighth Air Force which was equipped with British Lysanders and some American A-20 Havocs and A-35 Vengeances. The officer element of heavy bomber crews – pilots, navigators, bombardiers and radio operators, were trained at Cluntoe. Additional gunnery training at Greencastle was carried out at the Eighth Air Force anti-aircraft machine-gun school. There was also an air-to-air gunnery range off the north-east coast, near Cushendall, which was for use in cross-country exercises, subject to regulations and procedures which were the responsibility of the Eighth Air Force Composite Command HQ, which had to be notified 24 hours in advance of impending use, on receipt of which, RAF Flying Control was

informed. Firing was not permitted when shipping would have been endangered. In January 1944, use began to be made of a bombing target on Skady Tower Island in Lough Neagh which was constructed by the USAAF Ordnance Supply and Maintenance Company based nearby at Toome.

The training courses provided at the CCRCs were essentially of a top-up nature, to supplement the training that crews received in the USA where it was not possible to replicate the procedures and circumstances peculiar to operations in the European Theatre of Operations. Normally, they lasted between two and three weeks. Subjects covered included equipment, navigation, armament, bombing, gunnery, radio and RAF flying control procedures, airmanship, aircraft formation flying and forming-up procedures, tactics and intelligence which entailed the use of a wide range of facilities and is indicative of the intensity of the instruction provided. Records show that May through August 1944 proved to be the busiest period at Cluntoe, output in July alone being 330 heavy bomber crews. Toome's busiest month was August, with an output of 158 medium bomber crews which, it should be noted, went to the Ninth Air Force because when that organisation was re-located to England from North Africa in October 1943, it incorporated Eighth Air Force medium bomber units. Bomber crew training continued in Northern Ireland until September 1944 but, despite original plans, no fighter CCRCs ever became operational here.

11 US Naval Air Service

The decision by the US Navy in 1942 not to make use of Killadeas as a base for Catalina flying boats was by no means the end of American naval aviation in Northern Ireland. In October that year, keen observers of the scene at RAF Ballykelly might have been forgiven for thinking there had been a change of plan when a number of amphibious Catalinas appeared to have taken up residence. In fact, they were from the US Navy's VPB-73 Squadron, in transit from Iceland to Port Lyautey in Morocco to operate in support of the Operation TORCH landings in North-West Africa. Nonetheless, opportunity was taken during a short sojourn of several days at Ballykelly to continue the anti-U-boat patrols they had been carrying out with considerable success previously, sinking two and damaging additional U-boats over a period of seven weeks when they had been operating from Iceland.

In 1944, other US Navy anti-submarine aircraft again made use of Ballykelly. They were B-24 Liberators of Fleet Air Wing 7, operating out of their base at Dunkeswell in Devon. Four squadrons of FAW-7 customarily operated in conjunction with RAF Coastal Command's No. 19 Group which controlled all Coastal's airfields in South Wales and South West England. The Wing's main area of operations was the Bay of Biscay and English Channel but its aircraft could be called upon when and where necessary by other Groups such as No. 15 Group which controlled airfields in Northern Ireland and Western Scotland.

At the beginning of September, in response to the fact that U-boats had begun to operate in coastal waters of the UK in significantly higher numbers than hitherto, a new Battle of the Atlantic directive was issued which gave priority to RAF Coastal Command's operations in the areas of Cape Wrath, Northern Ireland, St George's Channel and the Bristol Channel. This resulted in FAW-7's Liberators being called upon to operate to the north and north west of Ireland and on nearly every day during the last three weeks of September, at least one, usually two or three and occasionally as many as seven

US Navy Liberators operated through Ballykelly and, on two occasions at least, RAF Bishopscourt. However, while their crews did obtain evidence of U-boat activity, including visual sighting and radar contact, no attacks were actually made, almost all patrols being logged as 'uneventful'.

Appropriately perhaps, the most sustained and intensive aspect of US Naval Air Service activity here during the Second World War was focused on the largest area of fresh water in the British Isles, Lough Neagh, at Sandy Bay south-east of Langford Lodge, between Ram's Island and the eastern shore of the Lough. This was the UK terminal for a scheduled twelve times weekly service operated by US Naval Air Transport Service Consolidated Coronado flying boats from and to the La Guardia terminal in New York, via

RAF Ballykelly
in October 1942

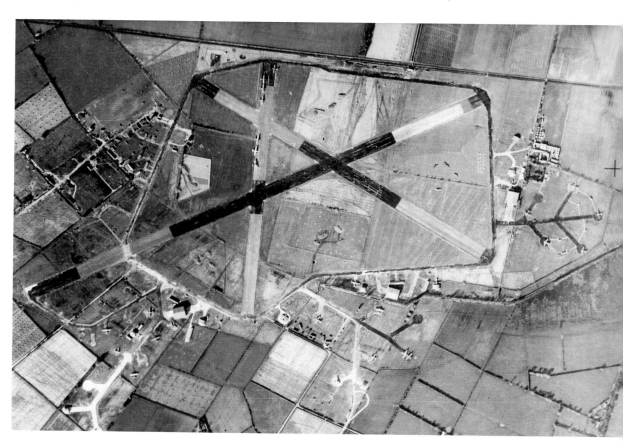

Botwood in Newfoundland or Shediac in New Brunswick or Port Lyautey in Morocco, this last transit stop being added in mid-June 1944 on a six times weekly basis only. The purpose was to convey personnel and urgently needed supplies and the operation came under the control of the US Navy Commodore at Londonderry. However, the RAF was responsible for the provision of accommodation and messing for transit crews and control staff in buildings that were erected at the residence known as 'Ben Neagh' close to Crumlin and Sandy Bay. Many of the Coronado pilots and crews were civilians seconded under contract by Pan American or American Export Airlines.

Coronado flying boat in flight

The service was part of the build up to D-Day and was inaugurated on 18 May 1944, when a Coronado arrived from New York, the first of 538 crossings of the Atlantic made by these large flying boats during that summer, the normal load being nine crew, between 10 and 18 passengers and freight. In the run up to D-Day, as many as 11 movements per day were recorded, yet only one accident was noted when a Coronado was holed on some rocks at Sandy Bay on 17 July. It was re-floated and towed to shore by the civilian McGarry organisation based nearby at Ardmore Boatyard, which maintained the moorings, using marine craft supplied by the RAF. Subsequently, it was repaired and returned to service.

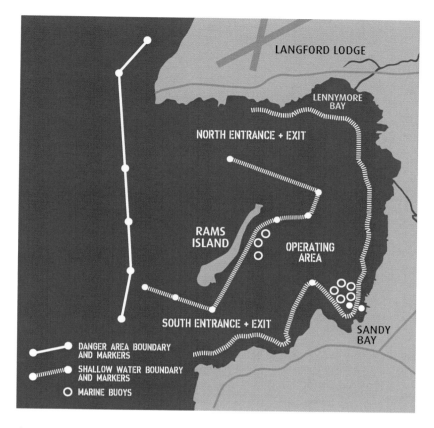

At a cruising speed of around 150 mph, transatlantic journey times were very slow by today's standards, lasting well over half a day, even on record-breaking occasions such as on 21 July when Captain Olaf Abrahamson of Pan American Airlines flew his Coronado between Sandy Bay and Shediac in 14 hours and 18 minutes. On 15 October 1944, all services were terminated.

12 Lisnabreeny Military Cemetery

It would be insensitive to conclude this brief account of American military aviation activities in Northern Ireland during the Second World War without mentioning a poignant aspect of the story. Reference has previously been made to the deaths of some American pilots in 1941 and 1942. Military flying, whether as a result of combat or active service, has always been dangerous and by the end of the war, almost 100 American aircrew had died as the result of flying accidents while participating in the various aviation activities that have been described, not only in Northern Ireland but also in Eire.

Lisnabreeny Cemetery in 1945

Virtually all the Eire deaths were a consequence of aircraft crashing during delivery as a result of becoming lost in bad weather, mechanical failure or running out of fuel. This applied also in the UK where hazards peculiar to flying training and intensive internal ferrying operations in all weathers were additional factors. The worst single incident occurred on 1 June 1944 and involved a B-17 Flying Fortress which was on transatlantic delivery by a combat crew, destination Valley in Wales, when it flew into Cave Hill whilst making a diversionary approach to Nutts Corner in conditions of bad visibility, killing all 10 crew on board.

It was not until December 1943 that the bodies of US Army, Navy and Army Air Force personnel began to be interred in the first and only US Military Cemetery to be established for the exclusive purpose, at Lisnabreeny, south of Belfast. From 12 March

Lisnabreeny Cemetery in 2013

1942, a small plot in Belfast City Cemetery had been used but by 7 October that year, when the 41st and last burial occurred there, the plot was full. Among the men buried there was 2nd Lieutenant Sharpe of the 52nd Fighter Group who was mentioned earlier. Between 23 May and 1 June 1944, all the bodies that had been buried in the City Cemetery were disinterred and reburied in Lisnabreeny. Between 7 October 1942 and December 1943, bodies were buried either in Northern Ireland, as was the case with the pilot Sergeant Fry, or shipped to England for burial in Brookwood Cemetery in Surrey.

By the end of the war, the bodies of 148 servicemen had been interred in Lisnabreeny, including those from the Cave Hill tragedy. In 1948, all were exhumed and either shipped home, if next of kin so wished, or taken to England for permanent reburial in the US Military Cemetery at Madingly near Cambridge. Almost half of the graves at Lisnabreeny contained the remains of airmen, including seven who were the victims of two B-24 Liberator crashes on the Isle of Man.

In 2013, a fitting memorial was constructed at the site by Castlereagh Borough Council, consisting of a granite obelisk on which are inscribed the names of all 148 men who were buried there. It is surrounded by a Memorial Garden, from which, poignantly, there are panoramic views across Belfast to Cave Hill and the site where the B-17 crashed. Within the Memorial Garden is interpretative signage and a flagpole from which *Old Glory* is flown on significant occasions.

Ernie Cromie

Unable to realise a boyhood ambition to become a military pilot because of defective eyesight, Ernie Cromie had a fulfilling career as a town planner but never lost his enthusiasm for all things aviation. He has been a member of the Ulster Aviation Society since 1979, serving as its Chairman for 30 years until 2012 when he relinquished all executive responsibility to devote more time to researching and promoting the history of aviation in Northern Ireland, with particular reference to the United States Army Air Forces and Naval Air Service presence here during the Second World War. He has written numerous articles for a wide range of aviation journals and other publications and is co-author of three books, this being his first solo effort.

If you have been inspired by this publication to take a deeper interest in the history of aviation in Northern Ireland you might consider joining the Ulster Aviation Society, which is an educational charity and can be accessed via the website – www.ulsteraviationsociety.org